Jo Simpson and I met at M.D. Anderson Hospital while each of our husbands were undergoing cancer treatment. We became friends who walked along similar trails exchanging our stories. Both of us realized the vital importance of the often unsung caregiver. Although the season has passed from "mourning to morning," Jo vividly recalls the impact and need to care for the caregiver. Passionately, prayerfully, and practically she equips and encourages the family and the love team for the journey. She fulfills the biblical mandate to "comfort one another." As you focus on those who are hurting, do not forget those who are helping.

Dr. Sheila Bailey
Author, *Makeovers with Leftovers*

In my forty years as shepherd of a diverse congregation (diverse in age, gender, ethnicity), it has been my task to provide pastoral care during times of distress and trauma. I have developed a passion for caregivers with whom I have come in contact. A key part of my passion for caregivers is driven by my realization that the ministry of presence is the greatest part of ministering to the needs of the caregiver.

I met Jo Angelia (Jo Ann) through her late husband, Rev. Dr. E. Thurman Walker, who began his preaching ministry under my mentorship. Our relationship was not only a mentorship in Christian ministry but also as best friends. Following our initial meeting in 1979 when Dr. Walker entered Christian ministry, I was a principal person in every major crossroad of his life, one of those being his marriage to Jo Ann on February 9, 1991. We would come together several times during the year either in their home city, San Antonio, Texas, or my home city, Colorado Springs, Colorado (also the city where Dr. Walker's mother and stepfather reside).

I received a call one night in February 2000 informing me that Dr. Walker had been rushed to the hospital with excruciating abdominal pain. It was discerned that a cancer located in Dr. Walker's intestine was causing the severe pain. Jo Ann and I developed a brother-sister relationship that grew closer as Dr. Walker's illness worsened. When Dr. Walker's health deteriorated to the point that death was imminent, my prayers, my concerns, and my visits to San Antonio shifted from church-related events to my constant concern for Dr. Walker's life expectancy and for Jo Ann's well being.

On one of my many visits, I asked Jo Ann, "Jo, how are you doing?" I explained to her that my reason for asking was that I am always very concerned about the person at the side of the bed, because in all of my forty years of pastoring I have noticed that everyone's attention and concern is focused on the person *in* the bed. The person *beside* the bed is generally experiencing hurt, fear, and disconnect—feeling unloved, unimportant, and unnoticed along with many other feelings that often can't be put into words.

I have also noticed over my years of pastoral care that generally there is only *one* person at the side of the bed. There are probably many reasons for this, but a few that I have heard are these: he/she does not want anyone but me, he/she does not want others to see him/her suffering this way, I am really the only one available who is knowledgeable and trusted by him/her, I feel it is my duty and responsibility to give the level of care and attention necessary, and on and on it goes. But the greater need is that of the person alone *beside* the bed. That person is suffering as much as and in many ways greater than the person in the bed.

Jo Ann was chosen by the Lord to write this book, from her experience of having done it . . . to help others go through their own caregiving struggles.

The Person Beside the Bed is extremely well written. I commend Jo Ann for communicating this critical experience in a very professional, practical, and personal way. I view the use of this writing as a benefit to a myriad of caregivers through an unknown number of years to come. I thank God Almighty for using Jo Ann for such a time and such a blessing as this.

I remind all caregivers of Psalm 121:1, which encourages you to look up to God for your help; all of your help comes from the Lord.

James H. McMearn
Pastor Emeritus, New Jerusalem Baptist Church
Fountain, Colorado

The Person Beside the Bed is a true-life experience of a person who portrayed genuine love and concern for the mate God had given her. And because this is an experience that so many are facing today, this book is an excellent help and encouragement. It is good to get firsthand information and not a how-to by someone who has not experienced the responsibility of caring for a loved one, a friend, or a relative.

This book has ministered to me as I have read it and recalled the occasions that I have had to see it in action. I recommend it to anyone who is the person beside the bed and for general reading by anyone who realizes that someday you may need some encouragement, love, and guidance along the way.

Dr. J. Carlton Allen Sr.
Pastor, New Mt. Pleasant Baptist Church
San Antonio, Texas

The reflections of my journeys with the pastor-prophet Dr. E. Thurman Walker are clear and alive. Those reflections even cause me to pinch myself back into reality. The call of Elisha was my call to "pour water on the hands of Elijah," as stated in the book of 2 Kings 3:11. Many have been called to great things, but the call to serve by walking, waiting, and washing is the greatest act any man or woman can perform. This same act is what Jesus performed among us then and even now.

This book shares experiences of a spouse, and those chosen like myself, who walked, waited, and washed on a consistent basis, while knowing the outcome, believing in a miracle, seeing and feeling the turmoil and pain, and mixing highs and lows to provide a joy for a moment of peace and comfort. It shows how we walked by faith, trusting that God would provide the strength needed for those moments, but we never gave up the hope of a miracle cure to bring back physical health and vitality. Yet in the end we matured because the one we were serving helped us to see Eternality through our service to Him. We never gave up, we kept the faith, and we viewed the transforming power of God.

May you be blessed by reading *The Person Beside the Bed*.

Rev. H. Fritz Williams
Antioch Missionary Baptist Church
San Antonio, Texas

THE PERSON BESIDE THE BED

Encouragement for Informal Caregivers

JO ANGELIA SIMPSON

FOREWORD
KENNETH R. KEMP, MD

CREATIVE ENTERPRISES STUDIO

BEDFORD, TEXAS

Published in association with Creative Enterprises Studio, A Premier Publishing Services Group, PO Box 224, Bedford, TX 76095. CreativeEnterprisesLtd.com.

Unless otherwise noted, Scripture quotations are from the Holy Bible, New International Version (NIV). Copyright © 1973, 1978, 1984, 2011. International Bible Society. Used by permission of Zondervan Bible Publishers.

Scripture quotations designated KJV are from the King James Version.

Scripture quotations designated NKJV are from the New King James Version, copyright 1979, 1980, 1982, Thomas Nelson, Inc., Publishers.

Library of Congress Control Number: 2013934043

ISBN: 978-0-9826143-6-5

Cover Design: Michael Gore, It's A Pixel. itsapixel.com
Interior Design: Inside-Out Design & Typesetting, Hurst, TX

Printed in the United States of America
13 14 15 16 17 18 MG 6 5 4 3 2 1

To

Informal caregivers everywhere;

My family, children, and grandchildren;

Mr. Roosevelt Bass Sr. (in memory of my mother, Thelma Raye Bass);

Myrtle Hemphill (in memory of Uncle Tony);

Roberta Bartholomew (in memory of Uncle Freddy);

The pastor and people of

Antioch Missionary Baptist Church,

San Antonio, Texas;

Mrs. Deloris "Mama Dee" Williams

and the memory of Oscar "Daddy Ray" Williams;

Mrs. Cophra Ann Rector and the memory of

Pastor J. J. Rector Sr.;

Ms. Patricia Bell-Casey;

Dr. Leo Edwards, MD, Michelle Griffin, and the Alamo Hospice;

The St. Philip's Community College Administration

colleagues and students 2000–2009,

especially my colleagues in the Social and Behavioral

Science Department;

Class members of "The Person at the Side of the Bed"

conducted the week of January 23–26, 2012,

during the Baptist Ministers Union of San Antonio and Vicinity

Thirty-Fifth Annual City-Wide Church Institute

at Maranatha Bible Church

CONTENTS

Foreword

There are few resources available to help caregivers who are charged with the task of supporting those nearing the end of life. We often look to the technical expertise of medical and nursing professionals to tackle the very difficult task of providing aggressive supportive care to the sick and dying. In recent years, the medical profession has increasingly recognized the service provided by hospice care in helping those with terminal illnesses, yet we sometimes overlook the fact that the caregiver—not just the patient—is also dealing with a life-changing situation.

Unfortunately, not enough attention is paid to the family members of those persons who approach the end of life—those persons who may have no technical expertise, who have gone through no specialized training, and who have never cared for the sick. The caregiver must navigate a maze of unfamiliar diagnostic terms, foreign-sounding medications, scary procedures, and strange persons from the health-care team invading their private spaces with probing, and often embarrassing, questions. They must all of a sudden become experts in medicine, spirituality, and emotional support—at least when it comes to their loved one's needs.

This book by Jo Ann Simpson provides an invaluable insight to the confusing world of a caregiver. As a devoted wife, she courageously and lovingly helped Rev. Dr. E. Thurman Walker transition from life on this earth to life in eternity. She was there with him every step of the way. In the process, she chronicled her amazing journey and shares with us in the pages of this book that we must care for the caregiver as well as the sick.

Rev. Walker was my pastor and my dear friend. As a physician and a minister who worked under his leadership, I watched Dr. Walker deal with excruciating pain, valiantly handle a terminal diagnosis, and endure anxiety and discomfort with each failed experimental intervention and each adverse effect from experimental medications. The care provided by MD Anderson in Houston, Texas, was good; but even more impressive than that, the care given by Jo Ann was outstanding. She has amassed a wealth of information to help others facing similar situations.

You will be blessed as Jo Ann shares with us the challenges and, yes, the joys of assisting those whom we love transition from this life to the next, knowing that Christ assures us an even better life in eternal glory. God bless you, Sister Jo Ann!

Kenneth R. Kemp, MD
Pastor, Antioch Missionary Baptist Church
San Antonio, Texas

PREFACE

Until the day we die, we will have problems and challenges. Caregiving requires us to adapt and change with the situation, and a resilient spirit allows us to recover and bounce back from difficulty. Resilience is crucial because change is constant. It doesn't mean you won't have negative feelings about life changes. Resilience is a matter of choice that requires practicing thoughts and actions that help you to press forward and endure tough times.

During a difficult time in his life, King David gave us an awesome demonstration of how to develop resiliency in 1 Samuel 30:6, "David *encouraged* himself in the LORD his God" (KJV).

My life has changed drastically since 2000, and I developed a saying over the past decade: "There is nothing constant about life except change and the fact that God does *not* change!" The role of caregiver was an experience that stretched me in ways I never could have imagined. As I look back on the experience, I thank God for resilience. I was able to cope with the changes. My constant mantra was and is, "This is the here and now. Live in the moment."

I certainly do not claim to have all the answers and have much more to learn myself. God placed on my heart to share the practical and spiritual nuggets He has shown me. I'm finding that many things I did instinctively as an informal caregiver were actions recommended by numerous professional resources provided for caregivers (many I have referenced in the book).

May God bless you! I pray that reading this book will be an encouragement for you.

Jo Angelia Simpson

ACKNOWLEDGMENTS

James McMearn of the New Jerusalem Baptist Church in Fountain, Colorado, Dr. Walker's pastor emeritus, who in October 2009 asked me the very pertinent question: "Jo, how are you doing? I am always very concerned about the person beside the bed." I pondered that comment in my heart as a topic I would one day pursue.

Rev. H. Fritz Williams, dean of the San Antonio Baptist Ministers Union, who asked me to teach a class. I asked if my focus could be "caring for caregivers." I took the opportunity to explore the comment raised by Pastor McMearn.

Dr. Leo Edwards, MD and his sister-nurse Michelle Griffin, who advised us and cared for us along the journey. The doctors and nurses we met at MD Anderson, especially in clinical trials and palliative care, became friends and were invaluable.

The many friends whose support and love was priceless, such as Cathy Brown and Darlene Lacy, who served as personal nurses; Patricia Casey (Pastor Walker's longtime friend and administrative assistant);

Acknowledgments

the rotation of Alamo Hospice nurses was amazing, especially Jade, who walked us through the "valley of the shadow of death" (Psalm 23:4 KJV).

Linda and Corey Ware (Pastor Walker's sister and nephew) were on hand to help in any way possible. I thank Deacon Dennis Ridley for working alongside Rev. Fritz and me to provide intense daily care for Pastor Walker before and even while hospice care was brought in. Rev. Frederick Smalls, who served as armor bearer to Pastor Walker from 2004 to 2006.

Pastor and Mrs. John Carlton Allen and family (San Antonio, Texas), Pastor and Mrs. L. A. Williams (San Antonio, Texas), Bishop James Dixon (Houston, Texas), and Pastor and Mrs. James H. McMearn (Colorado Springs, Colorado), who walked with us for years and stayed close.

Cophra Ann Rector, who was a role model for me as a spouse and caregiver to our former pastor The Rev. John Joseph Rector Sr. I also thank Pastor and Mrs. Kenneth Kemp and the entire Antioch Church family, who were unconditionally supportive.

I acknowledge the love, support, and great faith of my dad, Deacon Roosevelt Bass Sr. My aunts Myrtle Hemphill, Roberta Bartholomew, Barbara Bradley, and Betty Caesar were not only close during the illness of my mother, but also served as role models in how to be a loving caregiver to a spouse with a chronic illness.

I acknowledge and celebrate Mr. W. C. Simpson for his amazing show of love and support. As my husband in this new season of life, he has encouraged me to share my experience. His input as a family caregiver for his own mother, Mrs. Elizabeth Gordon, has been a source of encouragement as I have worked on this book.

Both T and Mom lived life intentionally and purposefully. They exhibited great faith and showed those around them how to live in the fullness of God's grace.

INTRODUCTION

In the United States there are more than fifty million family caregivers, providing an average of thirty-seven billion hours of unpaid, informal care per year for adult family members, children, and friends with chronic illnesses or conditions that prevent them from handling daily activities. Half of the US population has a chronic condition; forty-one million are limited in daily activities; twelve million are unable to work, go to school, or live alone. This research suggests that most of us, at some point as daughters, sons, husbands and wives, grandchildren, nieces and nephews, partners, and friends are likely to have some part in informal caregiving for someone else.

Becoming an informal caregiver can happen gradually or overnight. Often by the time people realize they are caregivers, they have already been performing the role for some time. The informal caregiving role includes varying levels from short term to long term, heavy to light duties, part time to full time, simple to light. Specific duties include but are not limited to buying groceries, cooking, cleaning, laundry, bathing, dressing, picking up and giving medications and injections, connecting feeding tubes, cleaning injection and IV sites, transferring someone in and out of bed, and transporting to doctors' appointments and therapies. Other duties include speaking and connecting with doctors and medical personnel, handling crises, making plans, and serving as the designated on-call family member.

Informal caregivers must adjust their time and lives to accommodate the needs of the patient. Family caregivers log in from twenty-one to eighty or more hours a week, and many do not get consistent help from other family members. Ethnic and minority family caregivers often put in even more hours. Statistics also reveal that many caregivers are elderly people caring for others who are elderly. Women make up to 75 percent of informal caregivers, although the percentage of male caregivers is significantly increasing. Five years ago the estimated value of the free, unpaid work of informal caregivers was at least $375 billion.

The length of the caregiving role is steadily increasing due to shorter hospital stays, shortages of health-care workers, home care technology, and longer life spans. Members of the "sandwich" generation (currently forties and fifties) are more likely to find themselves raising their teen children and caring for aging and ill parents. Caregivers over fifty are more likely to have been providing care for more than ten years.

As an informal caregiver, I was blessed by the testimony and encouragement of those around me who shared their stories, tips for survival, and who reached out to me in a very real and personal way. Every caregiving experience is unique, and each person has varied perspectives. My intention for writing this bookl is to encourage you by sharing my caregiving experience and the lessons I learned while carrying this "blessed burden." If you are currently in the informal caregiving role, have been a caregiver, know someone who is in the role, or it seems that your future could hold such a responsibility, I pray that my sharing will enlighten, equip, and encourage you.

Whether it's on this side or on the other side,
I am already healed.
THE REV. DR. E. THURMAN WALKER JR.
(1959–2009)

1

THE STORY

Lord, give me just enough grace for this day
to do what must be done and face whatever comes my way.
From Jo's Journal

Like most Christian couples, Rev. Walker and I solemnly took the vows that included the phrase, "in sickness and health, until death do us part." On February 9, 1991, we married, hoping for a long life filled with children, grandchildren, family, ministry, and close friends. We quickly realized that God had very special plans for our lives as He allowed unusual things to happen along the way. Most of those life events that we affectionately called "chapters" were welcomed and pleasurable while others were bitter pills to swallow. Yet swallow we did, always believing that God was in control and at the center of our lives.

One of the most difficult chapters began in February 2000 when "T," as I affectionately called him, was rushed to the hospital with a mysterious abdominal pain that nearly killed him. Through prayer and aggressive efforts by a team of doctors headed by our physician,

The Person Beside the Bed

Dr. Leo Edwards, and by God's will the source of the pain was found and resolved after four days. A tumor was found in his small intestine, and postoperative tests revealed that Rev. Walker had a very rare cancer called carcinoid syndrome. At that time the cancer was dubbed the "pretty cancer"—a very slow-growing and incurable form of cancer. Doctors in San Antonio and at MD Anderson Hospital (MDA) in Houston, Texas, gave us hope that the cancer, which had begun in the small intestine and metastasized to the liver, could be contained and treated. Cancer research at the time suggested that carcinoid cancer patients had a prognosis of from five to ten years if the condition was caught in the earlier stages.

From September 2001 until May 2009, Rev. Walker received an average of three new clinical trial treatments per year, as well as an ablation surgery on the liver in 2001. Immediately after the ablation surgery, T's pancreas was compromised, and he had to be fed nightly by a tube for four months. As time went on, the side effects from the clinical trial treatments were manageable and did not interfere greatly with Rev. Walker's ministry schedule or personal life. From the outside looking in, no one would have known the depth of the medical treatments and complications he was enduring. There were countless appointments at MDA, injections, pills, side effects, and ever-increasing symptoms. A real blessing in the midst of all that was that our medical insurance covered a significant portion of all the treatments, medications, and hospital care. However, there were times when I had to write letters and confront the insurance company regarding coverage issues, but in every situation God gave the victory and more grace. It helped tremendously that the actual clinical trial chemotherapy drugs were funded by MDA research partners.

As the treatments and side effects increased, our lives slowly changed.

I was so focused on helping T keep the medical side of his life as low-key and unobtrusive as possible that I really did not think about myself as a caregiver, but as a partner. He was adamant about not worrying the family or the church, and he was insistent about not allowing any of these medical issues to interfere with ministry obligations.

Along the way I continued to research T's diagnosis and keep up with the changing trends related to carcinoid syndrome. I tried to learn all I could so I could give the best support and ask the right questions during the MDA appointments. One of our challenges was that T was determined to use what time God gave him to accomplish ministry goals and projects, yet his medical condition was increasingly impacting his health and energy. Scheduling to go to appointments in Houston was a test of creativity and flexibility on the part of the clinical team.

Eventually we were required to be at MDA longer and more frequently. I was a full-time college instructor at St. Philip's College in San Antonio, Texas. The medical schedule caused me to have to use quite a bit of leave time and depend on the help of my colleagues. I adjusted by cutting back on my teaching load at the college and by taking more leave time. I did not believe in leaving a loved one alone in a hospital room or appointment where critical information would be given. It took two sets of ears and more to understand the complexity of dealing with an incurable disease.

During that time my mother, Thelma Bass, had been diagnosed with stage IV non-Hodgkin's lymphoma. In fact, she and T were diagnosed the same month in 2000. My mom was married to a wonderful man, Roosevelt (Sam) Bass, who was loving and supportive of her throughout her illness. I was an only adopted child, and it hit me hard to know that the woman who "birthed me from the heart," as she would say, the person who knew me best, was also dealing with a chronic and terminal illness. There were days when depression hit me hard. But I would look at my husband's and mother's strength and courage, reminding myself that if they could trust God with their lives, then so could I. I had no right to live with a defeated and doubting faith.

As the years progressed, Mom and T dealt bravely with all that their medical conditions presented. We were close as family, and we did whatever had to be done to get through—appointments, hospital stays, trips to Houston, rough mornings with slow starts, and all the while still living life, still taking care of children and walking with them in their seasons of growing up. Life does not stop just because someone is ill. People still lean on you, depend on you, and expect things from you. God gave all of us grace and strength.

During that time T lived intentionally and purposefully. He seemed driven to do all he could do with whatever time God gave him. He was a community leader, a pastor's pastor and confidante, and a loving shepherd to the flock God had given him at Antioch Missionary Baptist Church. He was also a wonderful father, devoted husband, caring son, brother, and uncle. He stayed in the Word and preached with ever-increasing depth and clarity. On this side of the experience, I see that he was trying to prepare our hearts and minds for the days to come. As he stood in the pulpit, I could often tell that he was having a cancer flush, which caused him to struggle to stay focused on what he was saying. I used to ask God to help the congregation to see with spiritual eyes the miracle in front of them and help them to hear with their hearts the messages T was delivering.

There came a point in 2007 when the daily ministry responsibilities drained T to the point of severe physical exhaustion. Due to the type of cancer he had, the endocrine system was compromised, and experiences that were adrenaline raising, such as preaching, negotiating, confrontations, and highly emotional interactions, would shut him down, causing extreme nausea, vomiting, and weakness. I began to realize that I was a full-time caregiver. About that same time Mom was also experiencing increased symptoms, chemotherapy, and decreasing energy levels, so I did my best to assist and support my dad. Like T my mother wanted me close, and I wanted to be there for her. I was honored to do what any loving daughter and wife would do, and with God's help things got done.

In October 2008 T began what would be the last of the clinical trials—the treatment that I believe ushered him more rapidly toward death. MDA clinical trial doctors consulted with us, gave us the options, and with our permission, began a series of arterial infusions of strong chemotherapy directly into the liver every twenty-one days. The treatment was so strong and harsh that T lost his hair the first week. It was surreal to see little clumps of hair literally falling to the floor as he walked down the hallway. Almost immediately his energy was zapped, and daily we had to adjust and readjust medications to calm the side effects. Within a couple of weeks, it had become so bad that the side effects had side effects! His daily activities and quality of life became seriously compromised. I would often cry silently while he was sleeping, asking God to show me what to do, tell me what to say, help me be bold and confident in making crucial and critical decisions.

By April 2009, during an appointment with the clinical trial team, I tearfully insisted that the treatment be stopped. I remember asking the clinical team, "If this were your spouse, your child, your parent, would you want to see him wither away in front of your eyes? This isn't right; there is no quality of life here!" I looked over at T, and he was furious with me, but in his heart he knew, and later admitted, that we had a small window of opportunity to have any quality of life, if only for a brief time. We realized that he was at the beginning of liver failure. No longer able to put T through treatments, the clinical trial team assigned us to the palliative care clinic at MDA. It was there that we met Dr. Donna S. Zhukovsky, whose expertise and compassionate approach won over our hearts and trust. After four months we were visited by an MDA social work case manager, and discussions about when to bring in hospice care began in earnest.

During May, June, and July 2009, T had a brief reprise of energy, not at the level he would have liked but more than he had been experiencing. In August progressive liver failure symptoms began, and on August 4, MDA released T as a patient. As we left the appointment and headed to the elevator, I remember thinking, *We are now the people we used to see walking down the hall after bad news.* No longer having to travel to Houston, our trips to Dr. Edwards's office or his coming to our home became a constant. I kept juggling medications, trying to stay on top of a new hurdle every day. During that time I wrote the following entries in my journal:

SATURDAY, JULY 18, 2009

We were supposed to be sailing for the Alaskan Inside Passage today, but we are at home. I truly believe that even in our disappointment, missing that plane was in God's plan. . . . I'm swirling with thoughts and feelings as I watch T struggle through each day just trying to muster up energy. I know the reality. Dr. Ajani said, "It's not good." After nine years this carcinoid cancer is showing its most serious and fatal consequences. The liver is "architecturally compromised." . . . I know in my heart his days are numbered; I know God is able; I know He is in control; I know all of that! *And* I know what I see before me. . . . I don't mind being a caregiver. I know if it were me that T would do the same. That is not to say there is not a serious adjustment daily, weekly, monthly as things keep changing. Medicines change, conditions change, levels of pain change.

My entry on July 18 was practical and matter of fact. It was how I saw things. At the end I said, "We are all dying daily." I expressed the way I saw the decline of his health:

TUESDAY, JULY 28, 2009

Even on this trip I have had to assist with bathing and dressing, but in his eyes and on his face I see the pleasure he feels being able to take this trip. Yesterday I had to look all over the boat for him . . . found him playing bingo . . . determined to get away from me! Sometimes I look at his body changing (every pound he's lost, I have gained, so I'm changing too!). The strong shoulders that seemed to bear everybody's burdens, as well as the weight of a church and community of people, have lost muscle tone; the bones are showing. . . . The strong legs that used to jog, play racquetball, lift weights—now swollen from top to bottom, heavy with fluid . . .

Eyes that could look at you, through you, bright with active ideas and able to see what others could not, now drowsy and dull from fatigue and medication. The voice that spoke with great clarity and conviction, purpose and authority balanced with tenderness, forgiveness, and truth is now slowed, interrupted, and sometimes barely audible but still there.

The Person Beside the Bed

Thursday, July 30, 2009

After missing the July 17 cruise, here we are on day 6 of a wonderful Norwegian Freestyle Alaskan Inside Passage Cruise—#1 on T's bucket list! I kept going back and forth with myself, wanting to go because everyone, even the MDA doctors, said we had to go now if we were going. We might not get another opportunity . . . but not wanting to go because I was afraid we wouldn't have a good time because he would be ill. But God . . . provided a way for us to go on this cruise sponsored by the Antioch family. In fact by missing the first cruise, we actually ended up with an upgrade—personal concierge, butler, and excursion assistant. Wow! Currently we are docked in Prince Rupert, Canada, but somehow we are not anxious to get off. The excursions have been fun but strenuous.

Monday, August 3, 2009

Better day. Leg swelling was down a bit. Seemed to have a bit more energy, appetite a bit better. Watched a lot of TV. Still fatigued but obviously feeling better. Then a steady flow of visitors from 6:30 to 9:30 p.m. kind of drained him. We were glad—pleasant conversation with family—but he was definitely drained. Didn't sleep well again, really complaining about the mattress (hardness). I helped him with a nice, long, warm soak.

Tuesday, August 4, 2009

Did okay, but appetite not good. Leg swelling still about the same. Skin dryness and dark spots seem to be increasing. I have been massaging his legs and feet daily with lotion to fight dryness. He wanted some BaySeas drumfish. Went to eat, and he did okay.

Then we went to find his "Marriot mattress." Evening time he seemed agitated. I laid down with him for a while, but he did not sleep well at all.

SUNDAY, AUGUST 9, 2009

Twenty years ago today T and I were actually on our first date! Twenty years later I am doing my best to help him stay on his feet. We missed church today; he was scheduled to preach. For the first time he didn't even fight the idea that he could not stand in the pulpit, let alone make it to church service. It's hard to watch this man of God, who loves church and loves preaching, not get up with excitement and put on his suit and tie. I know people are praying for him, for me. Caring and giving care is not hard; it's watching him lose his way of life to this disease as it seems to be reaching end-stage liver failure. I never thought this strong, busy, protective man would need my protection and strength to keep him going. It's hard watching a man who called his own shots, spoke his mind, and pushed a church and community to be their best now have to struggle to get a thought across. Shoulders that were broad and strong, that I and others held on to in good times and bad, in fear and in faith, now droop with fatigue and weariness, tired of being tired. But they are *still* strong shoulders because of all the people I know who have faced the battle of cancer and long-term illness, he stands shoulder to shoulder with them all! There is "a cloud of witnesses" cheering him on; there are people around him who, if they are paying attention, are learning to "fight the good fight!"

T transitioned from earth to glory on October 26, 2009. Exactly fourteen months later, on December 26, 2010, my mother went to be with the Lord. As I look back on those ten years, I have to admit that I did not know I was a caregiver initially. From 2007 to 2009 I was fully immersed in the role of caregiver. I knew I was a loving daughter and wife, and that two people I loved most in this life needed all the love and support I could possibly give. I knew I wanted to be a role model to my children and grandchildren by providing unconditional love and care to my husband and mother.

In the last nine months of T's life, a book titled *Farther Down and Deeper In*, a book posthumously completed by the late Pastor E. K. Bailey's wife, Shelia, and his daughter, Cokiesha Bailey (now Cokiesha Robinson) became a great source of encouragement to me as a caregiver. Both the book and Pastor Bailey himself had already been a source of strength to T. In 2001, during Rev. Walker's lengthy hospital stay at MDA, Pastor E. K. Bailey, who was fighting his own cancer battle at MDA, came to visit us. Rev. Bailey encouraged us by reminding us that whom God uses greatly He breaks greatly. Encouraged by that spiritual nugget, T found not only a spiritual role model but also grace and strength to continue.

During that time Pastor Bailey began penning his reflections about life, death, and ministry, which helped me to understand some of the emotional and spiritual changes T was experiencing. Sheila Bailey's thoughts and advice helped me to understand it was okay to ask for help and provided a guideline on how to structure our home for the inclusion of other people during time of need. She also stressed the realities of negative emotions and the challenges of keeping family together and communicating. E. K. Bailey passed away in 2004. In the years and months before he passed, we were graced to spend some quality time with Pastor and Mrs. Bailey. I highly recommend *Farther Down and Deeper In* for encouragement during caregiving.

In this book, I describe our journey as a "blessed burden." God is the Sustainer, Comforter, and Keeper! My constant prayer and mantra became, "God, give me enough grace and strength for *this* day to do what needs to be done and do it with love."

Chatter

Musings of the late Pastor Walker, which I recorded on July 15, 2009, 3:33 p.m. while traveling back to San Antonio from MD Anderson in Houston:

It's what people talk about—people talking through esophageal devices, overhearing people talking in waiting rooms, voices in the background, chatter with my doctors and other doctors. Our chatter has been over nine years. It's hearing God through other people and knowing God better through their chatter. "Be still and know that I am God." What have I heard God say?

I want people to know that I was healed since I was told nine years ago, "Oh death, where is thy victory? Oh grave where is thy sting?" Death won't have victory; the grave won't have a sting on me! Like anybody else, I think I've done my appropriate amount of suffering.

I can't go back on His Word. I am still healed. What's that old saying? "I walked a mile with Pleasure, and she chatted all the way but left me none the wiser for all she had to say. I walked a mile with Sorrow [cancer], and n're a word said she, but oh the things I learned from her as cancer walked with me."

You know, chatter.

Personal Notes

2

THE PRACTICAL SIDE OF THE BED

You may be part of that sandwich *generation—employed, caring for your children, running errands for your parent(s), and taking over chores.*

As we established earlier, every caregiving situation and experience is uniquely different. The temperament, personalities, and living conditions are all unique. The diagnosis, levels of care, and financial resources are also unique. Even the desire and level of commitment in caring for a loved one is unique. Millions of caregivers around this country, who nurture and care for their loved ones day in and day out, were thrust into the roles they play, while others gradually found themselves in it as I did.

As caregiver you have taken on a role that can give you a sense of pride, yet it is so stressful. At times family members may not understand or support your decisions. You may experience a role reversal as I did when the person who is now frail was the one who used to be in charge of the home business life. You may find yourself caring for a parent who needs your advice, comfort, and assistance. You may be part of that *sandwich* generation—employed, caring for your children, running errands for your parent(s), and taking over chores.

I did not read about this caregiving phenomenon initially. I read about the cancer condition to equip myself with knowledge, and I did research for any bit of hope for a cure. But admittedly, I did not read anything about being a caregiver. I had witnessed others in those roles, but ironically I did not associate myself with them. Yet as my responsibilities increased over time, I instinctively did some things that I now find, as a result of this project, were the right things to do.

Much has been written and researched about how to care for the sick, disabled, and terminally ill. As I explore this topic I will share with you resources I have found to be helpful. I never made a conscious decision to be a caregiver. I just saw needs and wanted to make things better for my loved ones. My research and reflection on the topic have given me the revelation that from day one in February 2000 when cancer became our diagnosis, I became an informal caregiver!

LEARN AS MUCH AS YOU CAN ABOUT YOUR LOVED ONE'S CONDITION

One of the wisest things a caregiver can do is to learn about the condition of their loved one. For me personally, spending time on the Internet researching T's medical condition was extremely beneficial. In the beginning it was learning the disease, the diagnosis, the treatments available, symptoms, side effects, and prognosis. Discussing what you find with the "care receiver" (patient) is essential. Some discussions may be difficult, but being informed and presenting a united front when visiting with doctors is essential.

In addition, you will find resources, such as websites and support groups, for nearly every medical condition you can imagine. Support groups offer informational talks and other caregivers share what they have learned. It is also a good decision to investigate *The Patient's Bill of Rights* so that interactions with medical personnel can be informed. I kept a detailed notebook with the results of appointments, treatments, and resources.

Evaluate Personal Finances and Make Adjustments

The communication about economic resources and personal changes in the home cannot be stressed enough. It is not wise to assume that things will just work themselves out regardless of your family income. Questions about medical and prescription coverage and resources, such as home health care and hospice, must be addressed. For caregivers and care receivers who are working, the discussion of available leave time is essential. Should the caregiver situation become more difficult, families may have to evaluate the economics of the primary caregiver not working in order to care for a loved one. Be sure to find out what your employer offers (e.g. FMLA).

Discuss Medical Power of Attorney and Legal/Health-care Wishes

No discussion is as difficult and sensitive as determining the legal aspects of who will make decisions for the care receiver. For example, if the patient is used to being the family provider and being independent, it can be devastating to give up autonomy. Yet a decision made with clear thinking and honest communication prior to crisis is a decision well made. For spouses these planned legal decisions can prove helpful when dealing with family members during a time of emotional crisis. It is one thing for a care receiver to express the desire not to be resuscitated, but it is quite another thing if the situation actually arises and there is no "do not resuscitate" (DNR) order and medical power of attorney authorizing the desires of the patient.

I also strongly suggest discussions include a will, living trust, statutory durable power of attorney and, if possible, preplanning for funerals. Many of us don't want to deal with such morbid discussions, but they are essential. You can alleviate the stress of handling a terminal illness and impending death by preplanning and avoiding potential family arguments and disagreements during the declining health and eventual death of a loved one. The focus of caregiving must be on the needs and wishes of the patient.

Include Your Loved One in the Decisions

This may seem to be advice for the patient, but it is really a help to the caregiver. When the patient feels included and involved in the decision-making process for as long as it is feasible, the relationship is strengthened. The one you are caring for has ownership in his/her own care and feels respected. Let your loved one know that you want him/her to have as much independence as possible.

When and if the time comes for bringing in professional (formal) caregivers, such as hired help or hospice, be honest with your loved one about what is needed, and allow him/her to express personal thoughts and concerns if able to do so. As a primary caregiver don't make unrealistic promises, no matter what! Assure the patient that you will remain the primary caregiver and that you will communicate your joint preferences. Make the loved one know that you will be clear with people coming in about who is the go-to person. Assure your loved one that you will give timely feedback regarding the persons working in the agency.

Discuss Your Needs with Family and Close Friends

The caregiver must learn to say yes and accept gifts and offers for assistance. The goal should be to get everyone who wants to be involved engaged in one way or another. You would be surprised how the simplest of chores can be immensely appreciated. I remember when my godfather, Deacon Oscar "Daddy Ray" Williams, was ill, and my responsibility was to keep him stocked with oatmeal! What an honor it was to be asked by his wife, Deloris "Mama Dee," to "make another batch of that oatmeal!" Wise is the caregiver who can make everyone feel special and involved during such a difficult season of life. When a caregiving situation presents itself, there are many who will offer their support and help. It is never too early to bring family together to discuss how the primary caregiver can be helped. It is easier to brainstorm about resources together. Use technology (website, e-mail, and texting) to keep everyone reminded and posted on their assignments.

Keep a calendar. There is a difference between being assertive and being bossy. The main caregiver must be clear about what is desired. Bear in mind that everyone has his/her own strength, so divide and conquer by matching up chores with abilities and availability. Pray for guidance and discernment about who to ask for help and who to include in your personal life. The reality is that you can expect hesitation or even refusal from some. I always say you can find out who's who and what's what during a time of family crisis. It is what it is!

Families can experience strain during a caregiving season. It is quite common for family members to want things to return to normal as quickly as possible when a loved one has been diagnosed with a medical condition. Temporary caregiving is one thing, but long-term-care needs by a family member can produce conflict and tear some families apart. As difficult as it may be, families in this kind of situation need to have regular check-ins to see where everyone is emotionally and to allow everyone's feelings to be heard.

Each member of the family has a unique relationship with the loved one, and a chronic or terminal illness can bring old family roles, frictions, and arguments back to the surface. Check-ins should be focused on achieving a family consensus and communication. Families should agree that the focus is the person who needs the care, so communication to heal emotional wounds is essential.

RESEARCH COMMUNITY RESOURCES THAT ARE AVAILABLE TO YOU

My knowledge of resources available to caregivers and care receivers grew as I took on this project. The services and resources of MD Anderson Hospital blessed and supported me as a caregiver. However, for those who are not or cannot be surrounded by such professional medical services, there are numerous resources available nationally and on the Internet. At the end of this book are a few of the national resources I ran across in my research. Reach out to others who have been through what you are experiencing. Many people are more than willing to share what they have learned. Don't hesitate. Ask! Ask! Ask!

Personal Notes

_____

_____

_____

_____

_____

_____

_____

_____

_____

_____

_____

_____

_____

_____

_____

_____

_____

_____

_____

_____

_____

_____

_____

_____

_____

_____

_____

_____

_____

_____

3

THE PSYCHOLOGICAL AND PHYSICAL SIDE OF THE BED

We must realize that even on our best days there is no such thing as perfection, and on our worst days we are probably doing better than we think we are.

Guilt is an emotion that can eat you alive! Yet it is a normal feeling. If you are feeling a sense of guilt, get help early and often to ease your load. Demands can eventually take a toll on even the strongest, most devoted caregiver. Perhaps you sometimes feel guilt for wanting time alone away from the patient. Perhaps you feel stressed because you are unable to meet the patient's unrealistic demands.

You can't be all things to all people, so set your boundaries. There is "good guilt," which results in trying to make things better; and there is "bad guilt," which produces nothing but ill feelings and strain. We must realize that even on our best days there is no such thing as perfection, and on our worst days we are probably doing better than we think we are.

Coping with Resentment

Often times a caregiver may feel resentment for the situation. Thoughts about the past, fear about the future, and frustration for things that may be lost along the way can consume you. Again, these feelings are quite normal, so do not feel guilty. The reality is that when we are caring for loved ones with chronic or terminal illnesses, things will not return to normal; many dreams and plans may not come to fruition as we once hoped.

Let go of a little of the past and a little of the future and focus on living in the moment. Acknowledge your resentment and find someone in whom you can confide—someone who won't judge you for the way you feel and will allow you to vent your deepest concerns and thoughts. Make sure that person is also able to speak the truth in love (see Ephesians 4:15), give balanced advice, and offer practical wisdom.

Coping with Feeling Unappreciated

There will be days when you won't feel appreciated, but daily remind yourself of the difference you are making. Stay away from the *shoulda, woulda, coulda* games in your mind, and remind yourself of your motive and intentions. I can tell you that if caregiving with purpose and passion could have kept my loved ones here, they would still be here! I reminded myself of that on difficult days.

Keep your eye on the big picture! The reward may not be in the external business of the day but in your internal peace, knowing you are trying your best to make things better for the one you love.

Coping with Feeling Overwhelmed

Caregiving can be an overwhelming experience packed with numerous negative emotions. A list of these emotions include denial, depression, anger, anxiety, panicky feelings, thoughts of your own death, nervous habits, withdrawing from others, loss of interest in hobbies, resentment, self-blame, blaming others, scattered thoughts, lack of concentration, decreased productivity, snapping or overreacting, feelings of helplessness or hopelessness, crying. There may be days when caregivers feel like withdrawing from others and avoiding friends and family. The reality is that there are some who love you but who don't know how to relate to you during this difficult season.

In that case reach out for help from family and consider professional help. The danger in allowing yourself to stay in such a frame of mind is that you may hurt yourself or your loved one emotionally or physically. Respite care is available as are other resources for caregivers that will educate you and assist you in managing these negative emotions. If you are a member of a church, this is a critical time to ask your pastor, minister of counseling, or a spiritual prayer partner(s) to come in and minister to you.

Coping with Feeling Angry

Do not expect that every day will be a good day, because the informal caregiving role has a serious learning curve. To deal with anger in a healthy way, acknowledge when you are depleted and sad. Snapping at others out of frustration is a warning that the situation has overwhelmed you, and you must focus on not beating yourself up if you experience an outburst.

It is the situation, not your loved one, that has caused the angry feelings. In order to cope consider breaking the huge responsibility into manageable chunks and give yourself permission not to think you are superhuman. Break down duties by the day, week, or month. Expect and plan for problems and issues that can arise for you as caregiver and for your loved one as the care receiver. At the end of the day, realize that whatever didn't get done that day simply will not get done, and it is okay!

Coping with Physical Issues

Caregiving is not a sleep-supportive situation. Sleep deprivation can be offset by creating a bedtime routine—activities that tell your mind and body that the day is coming to an end. Turn off the computer, relax with a bath, brew some tea, and settle down physically so that you can unwind mentally. It is important to let go so that your body can restore itself.

Caregiving is not an appetite-friendly situation. The mind, body, and soul are connected, so stress in your mind can lead to disturbances in your eating patterns. Stress may give you cravings for foods that are high in sugar and fat and low in nutrition. It is easy to grab fast food and junk that requires no preparation, especially when time is short or seemingly nonexistent. The result is sluggishness due to unstable blood sugar levels. Caregiving stresses can also interfere with normal digestion and lead to stomach disorders.

In some cases people will offer to bring food to the caregiver and family. Take advantage of these offers and ask for meals that are healthy. Force yourself to take time to prepare healthy snacks ahead of time, and be aware of what you are eating. Remember, if you are not good to yourself, you can't be good to anybody else.

Depending on the level and complexity of your caregiving situation, there may be heavy physical duties, such as lifting a patient who cannot assist you, bathing your patient in the bed, or pushing a wheelchair. One of the stresses I experienced was that I did not want my husband to know I was injured. I kept a shoulder injury to myself.

I felt that I alone was responsible for the lifting because T only trusted me! For months I neglected to get my shoulder checked despite a lump that would not go away. I also neglected my regular doctors' appointments because I felt guilty that I was relatively well. How dare I go to the doctor when my loved ones were fighting for their lives? Then came the day when T fell, and I could not lift him. It was one o'clock in the morning, and I panicked because I felt there was no one I could call!

The harsh reality fell on me that night—it was time for hospice. As a caregiver you have to give yourself permission to ask for help. When there is a danger of hurting yourself or your loved one, it is time to admit that you cannot do it alone. Give yourself permission to take a respite by finding a person you trust to care for your loved one for a few hours a week while you take time to tend to your mental and physical health.

COPING WITH ANTICIPATORY GRIEF

In 1969 the psychologist Elizabeth Kubler-Ross wrote *On Death and Dying* and proposed the well-known stages of grief as a way to analyze and assist people dealing with traumatic experiences in life. Her studies also inspired research on the occurrence of "anticipatory grief."

The stages of denial, anger, bargaining, depression, and acceptance are useful for this topic of caregiving and understanding your own and others' reactions to personal trauma and change, regardless of the cause. These stages can help you understand *why* time heals and *how* life can go on. Caregiving may or may not lead to the death of a loved one, yet long-term care for a chronic illness or terminal condition can lead to an anticipation of loss and a feeling of loss along the journey.

Grieve for your losses, then move forward allowing yourself to dream new dreams.

Resolve, Restore, Remember, Release

Celebrating the moment and living in the present can be healing for both the caregiver and care receiver. One of the things we tried to do as a family was find something to celebrate each day, including but not limited to birthdays, holidays, and anniversaries. We took more pictures, spent more time together with our children, grandchildren, and close friends, and we allowed ourselves to experience today's feelings. We resolved old issues, released old regrets, and focused on restoring a new and stronger relationship.

Caregiver Self-Assessment Questionnaire

How do you know when it's time to seek help for the care of your loved one in order to maintain your own health? A study of elderly spouse caregivers ages sixty-six to ninety-six found that caregivers who experience mental or emotional strains have a 63 percent higher risk of dying than non-caregivers. Caregivers are often so concerned with meeting their loved ones' needs that they lose sight of their own well-being.

Please use the following caregiver's self-assessment questionnaire to assess your need for help. Take just a few minutes to answer the questions beginning on the next page.

Caregiver's Self-Assessment Questionnaire

Check your honest response for each question.
During the past week or so, I have . . .

1. Had trouble keeping my mind on what I was doing.
   ❏ Yes   ❏ No

2. Felt that I couldn't leave my loved one alone.
   ❏ Yes   ❏ No

3. Had difficulty making decisions.
   ❏ Yes   ❏ No

4. Felt completely overwhelmed.
   ❏ Yes   ❏ No

5. Felt useless and unneeded.
   ❏ Yes   ❏ No

6. Felt lonely.
   ❏ Yes   ❏ No

7. Been upset that my loved one has changed so much from his/her former self.
   ❏ Yes   ❏ No

8. Felt a loss of privacy and /or personal time.
   ❏ Yes   ❏ No

9. Been edgy and irritable.
   ❏ Yes   ❏ No

10. Had sleep disturbed because of caring for my loved one.
    ❏ Yes   ❏ No

11. Had a crying spell or spells.
    ❏ Yes   ❏ No

12. Felt strained between work and family responsibilities.
   ❑   Yes   ❑   No

13. Had back pain.
   ❑   Yes   ❑   No

14. Felt ill (headaches, stomach problems, or common cold).
   ❑   Yes   ❑   No

15. Been dissatisfied with the support my family has given me.
   ❑   Yes   ❑   No

16. Found my loved one's living situation to be inconvenient or a barrier to care.
   ❑   Yes   ❑   No

17. On a scale of 1 to 10, with 1 being "not stressed" to 10 being "extremely stressful," please rate your current level of stress. (Circle your answer below.)

   1   2   3   4   5   6   7   8   9   10

18. On a scale of 1 to 10, with 1 being "very healthy" to 10 being "extremely ill," please rate your current health compared to what it was this time last year. (Circle your answer below.)

   1   2   3   4   5   6   7   8   9   10

Scoring:

To determine your score, total the number of yes responses in questions 1–16 and enter the number here: _____

Chances are you are experiencing a high degree of distress if your total score is 10 or more; you answered yes to questions 4 and 11; or your score on either question 17 or 18 was 6 or higher. If so, consider seeing a doctor for a personal check-up.

This assessment is adapted from silveradosenior.com/caregiver_self_assessment

Personal Notes

_____

_____

_____

_____

_____

_____

_____

_____

_____

_____

_____

_____

_____

_____

_____

_____

_____

_____

_____

_____

_____

_____

_____

_____

_____

_____

_____

4

THE SPIRITUAL SIDE OF THE BED

*I know God was with me, for when I look back
on things I did, I realize it was not me, but it was
Him working through me.*

For me the role of caregiver became a "blessed burden," and I maintained an attitude that it was my "calling"—what God was asking of me. It was both the best and hardest thing I have ever done in my life. As the stark reality became clear, I could feel God's grace more and more. The songwriter stated it this way: "Great is Thy faithfulness . . . morning by morning new mercies I see."[1] I know God was with me, for when I look back on things I did, I realize it was not me, but it was Him working through me. When I asked for wisdom about what to do about a medication, what question to ask at the doctor's office, how to organize my home, or who to include in the daily caregiving process, God gave me clarity of mind and courage to do what had to be done.

On one occasion T and I met with the palliative care doctors at MD Anderson, and I was asked to participate in a research project involving caregivers and a journaling project. I was excited about being included because journaling was one of my techniques of meditation. In order to be a part of the project, I had to answer a series of questions related to levels of depression and feelings of hopelessness. When the nurse assistant scored my test, she informed me that I was not "depressed enough" to be in the study. Wow! I was expected to be falling apart and distraught in my caregiving role. But I found my courage and strength in the Word of God in such passages as these:

> And let us not be weary in well doing: for in due season we shall reap, if we faint not. (Galatians 6:9 KJV)

> I can do all this through him who gives me strength. (Philippians 4:13)

> Do not be anxious about anything, but in every situation, by prayer and petition, with thanksgiving, present your requests to God. And the peace of God, which transcends all understanding, will guard your hearts and your minds in Christ Jesus. (Philippians 4:6–7)

"Lord, there has to be a blessing in obedience!" is what I would often say in my stressed moments.

On this side of the caregiving season, I believe God has blessed my obedience to Him as a spouse and daughter. The paradox of experiencing God's growing pains is that He gives strength when you think you have none left. There were mornings and nights when I went into the living room and on bended knee pleaded for God's mercy and strength. Each night was followed by a morning of peace, patience, and gratefulness for one more day with my loved one.

You can know all the practical and psychological answers, but as Christians we know that the only answer is Christ. Our lives have to be centered in Him and built on His Word. In the caregiving season I had to know God's promises and pray them. I had to believe Deuteronomy 31:6, which says in part, "He will never leave you nor forsake you."

The Bible says that the Holy Spirit understands and interprets our moanings and groanings, and He takes them to the throne of God for us. There was never a night when I cried out that God did not rescue my soul from sadness or despair. I do not know how people live through such an experience without believing in the Lord. The reward for our obedience and faith is God's honor! He does not forget our faithfulness. Without faith we cannot please Him.

HEAVINESS IS FOR A SEASON

"Thy shoes shall be iron and brass; and as thy days, so shall thy strength be" (Deuteronomy 33:25). In caregiving you will become tired, and you will become discouraged. Your emotional reserve will be tapped out. This course of life is a balancing act—a daily exercise in adjustment. No two days are the same. There are losses along the way. You may even lose a piece of yourself. There are days when your heart feels broken, but you must keep going; you have to keep doing what needs to be done. There will be days when tears will fall uncontrollably, but know that there is hope inside your tears!

There will be days when you cry out questions to God: "Why? Why me? Why him? Why her? Why now?" There will be days when He will be silent, and your heart will be heavy. Just know that when you can't see His hand, you need to trust His heart! When you stop asking why, you will hear God's voice and feel God's peace. You will be able to declare, not by your own power but by the power of God, by the power of the blood of Christ, by the power of the Holy Spirit, that God is good! In yourself, you will likely be weak and know bad days, but *in Him* there are no bad days.

My good friend Alice Allen, who is now a care receiver, has always encouraged me with these words: "God gives iron shoes for rough roads." Whatever your weakest physical, emotional, mental, spiritual predicament is, if you rest in Christ, God will always get you through. He has promised strength as long as your days shall last, strength as different as your days shall be—that's the promise.

You would not be human if you did not look at other people who are going through difficult experiences in their lives and say to yourself, "Please, God, I pray that I never go through that, because I don't think I could handle it!" Do you ever think like that? We all have things with which we think we would not be able to cope. I suppose in one sense you would be right, because you could not handle that "hard thing" in and of your own strength. *But God . . .* you need God's strength every day, and without it you are hopeless and unable to endure. If you draw upon God's strength and grace, you don't need to say, "I could never cope with this or that." The certainty is—the promise is—you will!

The reason you feel that you will not be able to cope if you ever face that heavy role is because you do not have that strength *today*. You don't feel it because you don't have it, and you don't have it because you don't need it . . . yet. God gives the strength you need *daily*, and when you have a day that needs that strength, God will give it to you! I can attest that I have gone through circumstances I could never have imagined I would face; yet I can look back and declare, "If it had not been for the Lord on my side, I'd have never made it!" The older seasoned folks in the church say, "He may not come when you want Him, but He's always right on time!"

The Lord *led me*, the Lord *helped me*, the Lord *gave me grace*, and the Lord *caused me to hope!* I'm stronger, I'm wiser, and I'm better!" What do you need? Do you need mental strength? Do you need emotional strength? Do you need physical strength? Moral? Spiritual? Whatever it may be, wherever your weakness lies, He gives strength to your specific need.

BE NOT WEARY IN WELL DOING

"Those who hope in the LORD will renew their strength. They will soar on wings like eagles; they will run and not grow weary, they will walk and not be faint" (Isaiah 40:31). You will seek comfort in the support of family and close friends. You will seek a moment of respite, of quiet time, just to step away for a while. But the reality of it all is that at times caregiving will be a lonely walk. People can only go a piece of the way. God plans it that way. You have to be patient and trust His process as you hope in Him and serve Him. Walk faithfully in the lane in which He has you. God has the opportunity to develop you spiritually and reveal to you the *what, how,* and if He so desires, the *why*. Whatever He decides, you'll understand it better by and by!

The apostle Paul described himself as the "least of the apostles" (1 Corinthians 15:9), the "least of all saints" (Ephesians 3:8, KJV), and the "chief of sinners" (1 Timothy 1:15, KJV), but as Paul's weakness became clearer, he remained committed to serving God, so God's grace blessed him more. That's why he says in Philippians 4:19, "My God will meet all your needs." Paul said in 2 Corinthians 12:9 that God said to him, "My grace is sufficient for you, for my power is made perfect in weakness." As long as you have demands and needs for strength, God will give His sufficient grace to meet your need. So Paul could say, "Therefore we do not lose heart. Though outwardly we are wasting away, yet inwardly we are being renewed day by day" (2 Corinthians 4:16).

Spiritual Truths and Advice

Finally, be strengthened by this promise: "We know that in all things God works for the good of those who love him, who have been called according to his purpose" (Romans 8:28). And be encouraged with these principles of caregiving as outlined by Carson, Knutson, and Witrogen[2] in 2004:

Believe that caregiving is a calling. Looking at caregiving as an appointed or God-given task makes it meaningful from the beginning.

Treat the mundane as sacred. Every task, from sorting paperwork to preparing food, can become meaningful if it's endowed with love and a passion to dignify another human being.

Maintain disciplines of reflection. Keeping a journal of thoughts and feelings, for example, can help caregivers become more self-aware and make them more likely to manage emotions better from day to day.

Pray or meditate. Contemplative practices provide time for much-needed quiet, outlets for releasing stress and connections to a wider universe.

Care for your body. Getting sufficient sleep, nutrition, exercise, and recreation help create conditions in which caregiving can be more rewarding than draining.

Repeat helpful truths. Saying the same affirming statements to yourself on a regular basis provides positive structure to a day and keeps the mind from slipping into destructive negativity.

Remember that attitude is a choice. Determine each day to view caregiving more as an opportunity for growth than as an undeserved burden. This sets the stage for joy and hope.

> *Whenever we focus on ourselves, it's not a spiritually healthy place to be. If my goal is to seek love . . .*
> *it comes from giving unselfishly, wanting the best for the other person, being willing to sacrifice for somebody else. Then you're not seeking a return, but many times, that's when the return comes.*
> —Verna Benner Carson

The spiritual side of the bed is a time of pruning and tuning, designed to make you better, stronger, and wiser. James said, "Consider it pure joy" (James 1:2) and give God the glory. If you can come to a place where you delight in a mature faith, you can give praise in the midst of struggles and trials, recognizing that God's grace is sufficient for you.

Let Go

Brothers and sisters, we do not want you to be uninformed about those who sleep in death, so that you do not grieve like the rest of mankind, who have no hope. For we believe that Jesus died and rose again, and so we believe that God will bring with Jesus those who have fallen asleep in him. According to the Lord's word, we tell you that we who are still alive, who are left until the coming of the Lord, will certainly not precede those who have fallen asleep.

The Person Beside the Bed

For the Lord himself will come down from heaven, with a loud command, with the voice of the archangel and with the trumpet call of God, and the dead in Christ will rise first. After that, we who are still alive and are left will be caught up together with them in the clouds to meet the Lord in the air. And so we will be with the Lord forever. (1 Thessalonians 4:13–17)

If your caregiving experience brings you to a situation where death is imminent, your faith should allow you to have a heart-to-heart discussion with your loved ones, if possible. It would be ideal if every situation resulted in the caregiver and family being able to "let go" with courage and full confidence that you will see your loved ones again. If we can hold on to the belief that God is in control of our lives, and the Scriptures confirm our destiny after death in the body, we will be better able to accept God's will for our loved one's life.

> *God will never let anything happen to you that*
> *you would not choose yourself,*
> *if you had known the beginning from the end.*
> —Delvin Atchison
> Pastor, Antioch Baptist Church, Waco, Texas

If you could know the blessing for your obedience at the end, wouldn't you choose to go through the trial?

Personal Notes

_____

_____

_____

_____

_____

_____

_____

_____

_____

_____

_____

_____

_____

_____

_____

_____

_____

_____

_____

_____

_____

_____

_____

_____

_____

_____

Notes

Introduction

1. Family Caregiver Alliance, "Caregiving." Last modified 2009. Accessed March 13, 2013. http://www.caregiver.org/caregiver/jsp/content_node.jsp?nodeid=2313.
2. Id.
3. Id.
4. Gibson, Mary Jo. AARP, "In Brief: Valuing the Invaluable: A New Look at the Economic Value of Family Caregiving." Last modified 2007. Accessed March 13, 2013. http://www.aarp.org/relationships/caregiving/info-2007/inb142_caregiving.html.

Chapter 2

1. U.S. Department of Health & Human Services, "Patient's Bill of Rights." Last modified 2012. Accessed March 13, 2013.

http://www.healthcare.gov/law/features/rights/bill-of-rights/index.html.

CHAPTER 3

1. The EKR Foundation, "Winter 2012." Last modified 2012. Accessed March 13, 2013. www.ekrfoundation.org.
2. Id.
3. Hanson, Polly. PBS, "Remembering for Two." Last modified 2004. Accessed March 13, 2013. http://www.pbs.org/saf/1402/features/remembering.htm.

CHAPTER 4

1. Chisholm, Thomas O. "Great Is Thy Faithfulness." 1923.
2. McLeod, Beth Witrogen. *Caregiving: The Spiritual Journey of Love, Loss, and Renewal.* Hoboken, NJ: John Wiley and Sons, 2000.
3. Carson, Verna Benner. *Spiritual Caregiving: Healthcare as a Ministry.* West Conshohocken, PA: Templeton Press, 2004.
4. Antioch Baptist Church, Waco, "Pastor Delvin Atchison I." Last modified 2010. Accessed March 13, 2013. http://hewittx.wix.com/antiochwaco.

APPENDICES

CLASS ACTIVITIES

- Ywata's Testimony

- Class Survey

- SCRIPTURES TO ENCOURAGE FAMILY CAREGIVERS

- Role-Play Situations

STATE LEGISLATIVE POLICIES FOR INFORMAL CAREGIVERS

GLOSSARY

REFERENCES AND RESOURCES

SELECTED WEBSITES

YWATA'S TESTIMONY

Did I want to go in or not? I had been praying for a safe environment to release my feelings, express my feelings, and feel and know that they were okay. A place that I would, in turn, get peace. My headaches and other symptoms were starting to get the best of me, even though I would keep pushing through, trying hard not to let anyone know of how much pain I was in emotionally and physically. Would I—could I—make it through these classes? I would sometimes have headaches so bad, and dizzy spells. If I made it through the work day, I didn't want to do much else. But here God was answering my petition. So as in the past, He gave me the strength to make it through. And when I look back, I know it was only in His strength I have once again pressed forward.

It was 3/6/11, 6:30 Sunday morning. I had arrived in New Orleans at 12:30 the day before, this time with my family and my sister and her family. But still I was the one Mom had requested to give her the meds and do the other patient-care type stuff. On this visit there was one new medication, morphine. We were now at the point of *comfort care.* Oh how I dreaded those words in my nursing career, and especially now. She had been refusing it before I got there because she wanted to be able to see her children and know them. And that she did.

But as the night wore on, her breathing became more labored. The restlessness grew, as well as the requirements for the morphine. I once called the nurse to ask what to do. How ironic that I, the nurse, was calling the nurse. I knew and agreed with her answer, but I needed someone else to tell me. "Increase the dose," she said. And I did.

It was that 6:30 dose that was too much for me. I gave Mom the dose. I held her close, rubbed her forehead, and told her it was okay, it would be okay. I then kissed her and left the room. I went and got my sister, who was awake and just lying in bed. We went to talk. I told her I didn't know how much time Mom had, but she was getting close. I didn't think I had it in me to continue giving her the morphine. I knew what it was, knew what it did, and it was just too much for me. In her calm social worker voice, she told me she understood. We agreed to call the nurses for further meds. As a good caregiver at 6:55 I was returning to check and make sure my meds were effective. As I walked to Mom's room, the phone rang. Who could be calling this early in the morning? It was Gayle, the nurse I had spoken to in the early hours of the morning. She said we were on her mind. I told her that I was on my way to check because I had just given Mom a dose. She said she would hold.

As I walked into the room, I wasn't ready for it, but it had happened. With the most peaceful look on her face, Mom had transitioned. Her body was breathless, no movement, still warm, but I knew even without a stethoscope that she was gone. I told Gayle, and she said she was on her way. Then I had to tell my family. I had to wake my stepdad, who was sleeping next to Mom, holding her arm. The first thing my sister said to me was, "You did good!" What could she possibly mean? I had just given Mom the last dose of morphine. How was that good? As the weeks and all the to-do list went on, family, friends kept saying, "You did good." I was at times ready to slap the next person who said that to me. I entered this class, and one of my reasons for being there was to find some peace. One night after a discussion, Sister Jo said to me, "You did good; you did better than you think you did."

No, I didn't slap her, but I realized that she meant it. She meant it from experience; she meant it from her heart, not knowing what I had been feeling. She meant it from knowing others' stories. I did good. I had always thought I was doing good, but for me it was that one last act that I held on to as the one bad thing I had done over the whole nine months. I had to release it. In talking to God I would say, "I am so glad You think I can handle this, because right now I am not feeling that way." And then a few hours later I would go back and say, "Thanks for trusting that I can handle this, but we are going to still have to talk about it. But for now thank You for the strength that I know only You can give to get thru another day." By the last day of the institute, I realized just how true it was that God knows how much we can bear. For He knew when it was time for not only Mom but for me. He heard and felt me at that time. We were granted favor the whole time because, no matter what, that was her appointed time. But God showed favor to us as a family in how it would come to pass. And I can see that. I know that. And I thank Him for that.

To this day of all the patients for whom I have cared, Mom will be my most treasured patient, and to know of all the nurses who could have taken care of her, she requested me. It's a blessing to have a faith-based environment to process this in/through. My prayer is in the success, healing, and blessing of those who will benefit from your "project."

Sincerely,

A person who has been at the bedside

Author's note: Mrs. Ywata Brown of the Antioch Missionary Baptist Church in San Antonio, Texas, was a participant in the January 2012 class, and this testimony was sent to me as an e-mail on January 27, 2012. I was so moved and inspired by this e-mail that I received her permission to share this with the readers of this book. I hope you were blessed as I was. Printed as received.

Class Survey

The Person at the Side of the Bed
Encouragement for Informal Caregivers

This survey was designed by Jo A. Simpson, M. A. Sociology, based on the curriculum material and administered prior to the beginning of the class taught January 23–26, 2012.

1. Are you currently a caregiver for a loved one?
2. If you answered yes to question 1, what is the relation of the family member to you?
3. How long have you been in this role?
4. Do you know someone in or outside of your family who is a primary, informal caregiver?
5. If you answered yes to question 4, do you have a role in assisting that individual?
6. What do you believe are the top three issues informal caregivers face in caring for a loved one?
7. Does your church have a ministry that focuses on caregivers?
8. Have you or someone you know ever participated in a support group for caregivers?
9. What do you hope to gain as a result of taking this class?
10. On the last day of this class, we want to distribute a list of scriptures to share beyond these walls to encourage caregivers who are distressed and grieving. Please write a scripture below that you have leaned on and/or believe will encourage someone who is in the season of caregiving. Feel free to write more than one.

Class Survey

What do you believe are the top three (3) issues informal caregivers face when caring for a loved one?

- They feel burned out.
- They are dissatisfied with family support.
- They are under stress.
- Patience.
- Financial issues. Personal expenses.
- Balancing time between personal family members. Time for spouse. Not enough time. Juggling your schedule.
- Physical, emotional, health strains.
- Trying to keep the care receiver from being discouraged.
- Listening carefully when they are trying to say something.
- Trying to understand their frustration.
- Transportation.
- Medication. Knowledge of the diagnosis and how to take care of them. Proper training to deal with the situation.
- Administering medication and understanding the side effects.

Responses to Item 10 on the Caregiver Survey

Please see the Scriptures on the following pages.

Scriptures to Encourage Family Caregivers

Compiled by class members of "The Person Beside the Bed"
during the week of January 23–26, 2012
Baptist Ministers Union of San Antonio and Vicinity
Thirty-Fifth Annual City-Wide Church Institute
Maranatha Bible Church

Matthew 5:4 (KJV)

Blessed are they that mourn: for they shall be comforted.

Isaiah 40:28–31 (KJV)

Hast thou not known? hast thou not heard, that the everlasting God, the LORD, the Creator of the ends of the earth, fainteth not, neither is weary? there is no searching of his understanding. He giveth power to the faint; and to them that have no might he increaseth strength. Even the youths shall faint and be weary, and the young men shall utterly fall: But they that wait upon the LORD shall renew their strength; they shall mount up with wings as eagles; they shall run, and not be weary; and they shall walk, and not faint.

Isaiah 41:10 (KJV)

Fear thou not; for I am with thee: be not dismayed; for I am thy God: I will strengthen thee; yea, I will help thee; yea, I will uphold thee with the right hand of my righteousness.

Isaiah 54:17 (KJV)

No weapon that is formed against thee shall prosper; and every tongue that shall rise against thee in judgment thou shalt condemn. This is the heritage of the servants of the Lord, and their righteousness is of me, saith the Lord.

Isaiah 55:8 (KJV)
For my thoughts are not your thoughts, neither are your ways my ways, saith the Lord.

Malachi 4:2 (KJV)
But unto you that fear my name shall the Sun of righteousness arise with healing in His wings; and ye shall go forth, and grow up as calves of the stall.

Philippians 1:6 (KJV)
Being confident of this very thing, that he which hath begun a good work in you will perform it until the day of Jesus Christ.

Philippians 1:21 (KJV)
For to me to live is Christ, and to die is gain.

Philippians 4:6–7 (KJV)
Be careful for nothing; but in everything by prayer and supplication with thanksgiving let your requests be made known unto God. And the peace of God, which passeth all understanding, shall keep your hearts and minds through Christ Jesus.

1 Peter 3:12–14 (NKJV)
For the eyes of the Lord are on the righteous, And His ears are open to their prayers; But the face of the Lord is against those who do evil. And who is he who will harm you if you become followers of what is good? But even if you should suffer for righteousness' sake, you are blessed. "And do not be afraid of their threats, nor be troubled."

Scriptures to Encourage Family Caregivers

1 Peter 5:7 (KJV)
Casting all your care upon Him; for he careth for you.

Proverb 3:6 (NKJV)
In all your ways acknowledge Him, and He shall direct your paths.

Psalm 23 (NKJV)
The Lord is my shepherd; I shall not want. He makes me to lie down in green pastures; He leads me beside the still waters. He restores my soul; He leads me in the paths of righteousness for His name's sake. Yea, though I walk through the valley of the shadow of death, I will fear no evil; for You are with me; Your rod and Your staff, they comfort me. You prepare a table before me in the presence of my enemies; You anoint my head with oil; my cup runs over. Surely goodness and mercy shall follow me All the days of my life; and I will dwell in the house of the Lord forever.

Psalm 37:4 (NKJV)
Delight yourself also in the Lord, and He shall give you the desires of your heart.

Psalm 37:23–24 (NKJV)
The steps of a good man are ordered by the Lord, and He delights in his way. Though he fall, he shall not be utterly cast down; for the Lord upholds him with His hand.

Psalm 92:12–13 (NKJV)
The righteous shall flourish like a palm tree, he shall grow like a cedar in Lebanon. Those who are planted in the house of the Lord shall flourish in the courts of our God.

Psalm 100:3 (KJV)

Know ye that the Lord he is God; it is he that made us, and not we ourselves, we are his people, and the sheep of his pasture.

Psalm 103:3 (KJV)

Who forgiveth all thine iniquities; who healeth all thy diseases.

Psalm 121 (NKJV)

I will lift up my eyes to the hills—from whence comes my help?
My help comes from the LORD, who made heaven and earth.

He will not allow your foot to be moved; He who keeps you will not slumber. Behold, He who keeps Israel shall neither slumber nor sleep.

The LORD is your keeper; the LORD is your shade at your right hand. The sun shall not strike you by day, nor the moon by night.

The LORD shall preserve you from all evil; he shall preserve your soul. The LORD shall preserve your going out and your coming in from this time forth, and even forevermore.

Psalm 134:2 (NKJV)

Lift up your hands in the sanctuary, and bless the LORD.

1 Thessalonians 5:16–18 (NKJV)

Rejoice always, pray without ceasing, in everything give thanks; for this is the will of God in Christ Jesus for you.

ROLE-PLAY SITUATIONS

During the class students participated in role-play situations designed to help develop skills in responding spiritually to those informal caregivers in need of encouragement. The experience allowed students to see where they were personally, depending on their experiences. All of the students in this course were either in the informal caregiver role, knew someone who was currently in the role, or had been in the role previously. All situations were created by the author/teacher based on personal experiences.

ROLE-PLAY SITUATION 1

You are in the grocery store and run into a person from your church whom you have not seen for some time. You greet each other, and in the course of conversation you find out that this person has been thrust into an informal caregiving role. The person seems very distraught and discouraged. How will this conversation go? How do you encourage him/her personally? What are some things you can do after you walk away from this conversation?

ROLE-PLAY SITUATION 2

One of your parents is ill. There is a supervisor on your job who keeps giving you a hard time because you had to cut back on hours and/ or miss work altogether. No matter what explanations you give, this person does not seem to care about your situation and makes the work environment miserable. This is adding to your stress and making you deal with several negative emotions that are impacting your work, your spirit, and your caregiving demands. How can you deal with this situation to create a positive outcome?

ROLE-PLAY SITUATION 3

You are in the waiting room while your care receiver is taking yet another test! You sit behind a person who is talking to someone else. That person is expressing anger about the terminal diagnosis of her loved one. While she is venting you hear her say she has no one to turn to for help, she has a feeling of utter hopelessness, and everyone who started out helping has disappeared. To make matters worse, you hear her say she finds it hard to believe in a God who would allow these things to happen. Others around the room hear the same thing but turn away as if they don't want to get involved. What do you do?

ROLE-PLAY SITUATION 4

A friend of yours is cast into the caregiving role, and you notice that he is not taking care of himself physically. All efforts to encourage him to get some help have been refused. His loved one has insisted on total privacy, but you see that your friend is overwhelmed emotionally and spiritually—on the verge of a meltdown. What can you do or say to ultimately convince your friend that he needs physical and spiritual respite?

State Legislative Policies

How can I find out about state legislative policies that can help me as an informal family caregiver?

During the teaching of this class in January 2012, I was blessed to have the Honorable Senator Ciro Rodriguez, of San Antonio, Texas, as a class member. During our week of discussions, Mr. Rodriguez enlightened all of us and raised our awareness on the issue of informal caregiving from a political perspective.

Being a man of the people, Senator Rodriguez shared with the class his own experience with the role of caregiving. He went on to encourage the author to seek out and share the policies that Texas had to provide financial assistance for informal caregivers in an effort to reduce some of the stresses of caring for a loved one.

This book is designed to help people who may be from any part of the United States. The following websites help the reader to access pending, adopted, and current legislature specifically aimed at informal family caregivers. Caregiver awareness is strengthened by the wealth of articles, documents, state caregiving policy briefs, state profiles, statutes, constitutions, audits, and research reports. Many of these references cover the impact of Obamacare on informal family caregivers. Look up the following for yourself or someone you know in the caregiving season:

- Family Caregiver Alliance (www.caregiver.org) Caregiving Policy Digest available from website.
- Helping You Care (http://www.HelpingYouCare.com) A Comprehensive Family Caregiver's Resource
- National Conference of State Legislatures (www.ncsl.org/issue)

GLOSSARY

Blue Book (Listing of Impairments): The Social Security publication that provides detailed information about disability programs to physicians and other health care professionals. The Blue Book includes the complete "Listing of Impairments," which lists and defines those conditions considered severe enough to prevent a person from doing any gainful activity. The Blue Book can now be accessed online.

Care Manager/Case Manager: A social worker, nurse, or other professional who assesses needs and helps families plan and arrange informal and formal services.

Do Not Resuscitate Order (DNR): A code or order usually appearing in a patient's medical record indicating that, in the event the heart and/or breathing stops, no intervention be undertaken by staff. Death occurs undisturbed. This does not mean that the individual does not receive care. Continuing care is provided as it would to any individual (medications for pain, antibiotics, and the like), except as stated above.

Durable Power of Attorney: A Power of Attorney not affected by subsequent disability of the individual.

Home Health Agency (HHA): A public or private agency certified by Medicare that specializes in providing skilled nurses, homemakers, home health aides, and therapeutic services, such as physical therapy or occupational therapy, in an individual's home.

Home Health Care Services: Assistance covered by Medicare that include part-time or periodic skilled nursing care; home health aide services; physical therapy; occupational therapy; speech-language therapy; medical social services; durable medical equipment, such as wheelchairs, hospital beds, oxygen, and walkers; medical supplies; and other services.

Glossary

Hospice Care Services are covered by Medicare Part A for individuals with a terminal illness. Services may include prescriptions for symptom control and pain relief, medical and support services from a Medicare-approved hospice, and other services not otherwise covered by Medicare. Hospice care is usually given in an individual's home; however, Medicare may cover some short-term hospital and inpatient respite care (care given to a hospice patient so that the usual caregiver can rest).

Homemaker or Home Health Aide: A person who is paid to help in the home. Agencies make a distinction between homemaking (or housekeeping) services and personal care services.

Incapacitated Adult: A legally incapacitated person is someone who is impaired by sickness, accident, injury, mental illness, mental disability, chronic use of drugs, chronic intoxication, or any other cause, to the extent that the person does not have sufficient understanding or ability to make or communicate responsible decisions concerning his/her day-to-day care.

In-Home Supportive Services (IHSS): A program that provides domestic, paramedical, and personal assistance services for people with disabilities so that they can live independently or maintain employment safely. The IHSS program provides an alternative to living in an institution for many people.

Living Will: A document that describes a person's wishes with respect to the use of heroic life support measures to maintain life.

Long-Term Care: Services that assist individuals with long-term medical and personal needs. Long-term care may include medical services, physical therapy, custodial care, and assistance with activities of daily living (dressing, eating, bathing). Long-term care may be provided at home, in the community, or in facilities, including nursing homes and assisted-living facilities. Medicare will not pay exclusively for custodial care.

Long-Term Disability (LTD): LTD is an income replacement program that protects you and your family in the event you become disabled and are unable to perform the material and substantial duties of your job.

Long-Term Care: A term used to represent a range of services that address the health, social, and personal care needs of individuals delivered over a long period of time to persons who have never developed or have lost some capacity for self-care.

Medicare Advantage: A Medicare program that offers benefits by private insurance companies. These plans can provide more choices and extra benefits. Medicare Advantage Plans include: Managed Care (Medicare HMOs), Private Fee-for-Service, Preferred Provider Organization, and Special Needs Plans. Everyone who has Medicare Parts A and B is eligible to join a plan, except most people with End-Stage Renal Disease (ESRD).

Paramedical Services: Services that are prescribed by a doctor and often administered by in-home care providers. They typically require some level of training or judgment and are essential to the health of the recipient. Common examples include injections, administration of medication, catheter insertion and care, tube feeding, ventilator and oxygen care, treatment of wounds, and other services requiring sterile procedures.

Permanently and Totally Disabled: Unable to engage in any Substantial Gainful Activity (SGA) due to any medically determinable physical or mental impairment(s) which can be expected to result in death or which have lasted or can be expected to last for a continuous period of at least twelve months.

Power of Attorney: The simplest and least expensive legal device for authorizing a person to manage the affairs of another. In essence, it is a written agreement, usually with a close relative, an attorney, business associate or financial advisor, authorizing that person to sign documents and conduct transactions on the individual's behalf. The individual can delegate as much or as little power as desired and end the arrangement at any time.

Protective Supervision: Monitoring the activities of a person with cognitive disabilities to ensure that they are not a harm to themselves or others.

Spend Down: Under the Medicaid program, a method by which an individual establishes Medicaid eligibility by reducing gross income through incurring medical expenses until net income (after medical expenses) meets Medicaid financial requirements. A resident spends down when he/she is no longer sufficiently covered by a third-party payer (usually Medicare) and has exhausted all personal assets. The resident then becomes eligible for Medicaid coverage.

Note: The terms included in this glossary were compiled from the following public resource websites:

(www.agingcarefl.org/caregiver)

(www.thefamilycaregiver.org)

References and Resources

Area Agency on Aging. *For Caregivers: Handbook and Resource Guide.* Retrieved January 12, 2012. Agingcare.org.caregiver/fourstages agis.com/eldercare

Economic Value of Informal Caregivers. Retrieved January 12, 2012. www.assets.aarp.org

E. K. Bailey, Shelia Bailey, and Cokeshia Bailey. *Farther Down and Deeper In* (Chicago: Moody, 2005).

Hubpages. *What Is Caregiver Burnout?* (83) Retrieved January 9, 2012. www.caregiver.com

Leeza Gibbons, *Caregiver Confessions: Firsthand Advice from a Caregiver Who's Been There.* Retrieved January 22, 2012. www.caring.com

Verna Benner Carson, *Spiritual Caregiving: Healthcare as a Ministry* (West Conshohocken, PA: Templeton, 2004).

"Women Do the Heavy Lifting!" Selected caregiver statistics fact sheet. www.defenderofcaregivers.com

Leonor Crossley, "What is the definition of caregiving?" www.eHow.com

Family Caregiver Alliance. National Center on Caregiving. Retrieved January 12, 2012. www.caregiver.org

Elizabeth Kubler-Ross, *On Death and Dying.* (Farmington Hills, MI: Charles Scribner & Sons, 1997).

References and Resources

Beth Witrogen McLeod, *Caregiving: The Spiritual Journey of Love, Loss, and Renewal.* (Hoboken, NJ: John Wiley and Sons, 2000).

Jeffrey G. Macdonald, "Burdens as Blessings: Lessons on how a spiritually rich life can become the heart of caregiving." Retrieved January 9, 2012. www.caringtoday.com/reduce-stress/burdens-as-blessings

Alzheimer's Disease Patient Caregiver Guide. Retrieved January 12, 2012. www.medicinenet/alzheimers.com

Marsha Mailik Seltzer and Lydia Wailing Li, *The Transitions of Caregiving: Subjective and Objective Definitions.* (The Gerontological Society of America, 1996)

National Family Caregivers Association. thefamilycaregiver.org

Selected Websites

Be Smart. Be Well is a health and wellness website designed to raise awareness of largely preventable health and safety issues. Explore engaging video stories about real family caregivers and family caregiving experts, including Suzanne Mintz, president and cofounder of the National Family Caregivers Association. The videos highlight the highly personal and profound struggles of caregivers and how they can also bring families together. Other videos show how caregiver stress can take a heavy toll on the caregivers and ways to cope with the stress for your own health and well-being. http://besmartbewell.com/caregiving/index.htm

CareCentral CareCentral is a personalized web service that allows users to create a private, secure online community for loved ones during significant health events. It is a free tool to update friends and family, organize and schedule offers to help, and encourage messages of hope, providing support when it is most needed. http://www.carecentral.com

CarePages are free, private Web pages that make it easy to reach out and receive messages of support and to stay connected to family, friends, coworkers, and others who care about you and your loved one. The service is available to anyone caring for a loved one, but it may be particularly helpful to those who have recently found themselves in a caregiving role. http://www.carepages.com

Eldercare Locator National Association of Area Agencies on Aging provides referrals to area agencies on aging via zip code locations. Family caregivers can also find information about many eldercare issues and services available in local communities. http://www.eldercare.gov

Selected Websites

Lotsa Helping Hands is a free online service for creating private caregiving coordination communities where family and friends can stay informed and more easily provide assistance and support to caregivers. The service features many communication and social networking tools, including the ability to easily store and retrieve vital medical, financial, and contact information, convey medical updates, and post photos. In addition the easy-to-use calendar is specifically designed for organizing helpers where everyone can pitch in with meal deliveries, rides, visits, and other tasks. http://www.nfca.lotsahelpinghands.com

RxCompare is a free tool developed by Medicare Access for Patients-Rx (MAPRx) to help users determine if they need to enroll in a Medicare drug plan and, if they do, to systematically compare the drug plans where they live and select the best option for their prescription needs. RxCompare works in tandem with Medicare's on-line "Prescription Drug Plan Finder" and with information available from plans or 1-800-MEDICARE. http://www.maprx.info

Video Caregiving is a visual education tool for family caregivers of loved ones with Alzheimer's disease, strokes, or other physical disabilities. The site features exclusive documentary-style videos, created by a team of award-winning film producers, that follow real-life people as real-life stories and issues unfold. Here caregivers find tools to better understand and deal with their situations, and let them know that they are neither isolated nor alone in their struggle. http://www.videocaregiving.org.

ABOUT THE AUTHOR

Jo Angelia Simpson was born in Salzburg, Austria, in 1958— "God's gift" birthed into the hearts of a young military couple, Joseph Curtis and Thelma Raye Waters.

Thelma Bass was a loving wife, mother, and educator. Above all she was a role model for Christian women, young and old. Jo says, "Much of who I am as a person, and what I did as a caregiver, are because of the unconditional love Mom gave to her family, church, and community. I cherish her legacy."

Jo began her teaching career in 1980, and her experience in the secondary and elementary classroom have shaped and confirmed her love of teaching and transforming lives. In 1996, after earning a Master of Arts in Teaching Sociology with a minor in Psychology from Texas State University, Jo served as an instructor of Sociology at St.

Philip's Community College in San Antonio, Texas, from January 1997 to January 2012. Jo continues to touch lives in the classroom as an adjunct instructor at Cincinnati State Technical and Community College.

In 1989 Jo Angelia joined the Antioch Missionary Baptist Church, and in 1991 married Rev. E. Thurman Walker Jr., who became senior pastor of Antioch in 1993. She worked beside her pastor-husband in ministry to the church and community until the Lord called Pastor Walker home on October 26, 2009, after a nine-year battle with cancer.

During the years at Antioch, Jo developed her spiritual gifts through puppet ministry, working with youth in Sunday school, teaching New Member Orientation, Vacation Bible School, college ministry, Rites-of-Passage, and national youth conventions.

Jo Angelia has written and directed two plays: *The Miracle of Christmas* (1995); and *How Ruth Got Her Praise Back* (1999–2000). She participated as a writer of Sunday school material from 2007 to 2008. Jo has been a popular speaker and teacher for the San Antonio area churches and possesses the gift of encouragement as she shares what God has done in and through her life.

Jo has been instrumental in the development of the Walker Institute of Learning and Leadership for Boys of Excellence (known as The WILL BE Academy) in San Antonio. The school is focused on the academic success and spiritual development of middle school boys and is the vision of the late Pastor Walker. Jo has also served as a volunteer at MD Anderson Hospital in Houston, Texas, offering a tender hand and heart as a caregiver.

In July 2011 Jo married Mr. W. C. Simpson, whom she describes as her "blessing from God for my obedience to Him." He has been best friend, encourager, and "the wind beneath my wings." She is currently a member of the Inspirational Baptist Church City of Destiny in Cincinnati, Ohio, where Bishop Victor S. Couzens is senior pastor. Jo is the founder of PalmTreeWoman Ministries, which is designed to reach out to all Christians, women in particular, inspiring them to be strong in their faith walk.

As a mother, the joys of her heart are her children: Taliferro Neal Jr (Clarissa), and daughter, Kimberly Marie Benford Johns (Karl), and a host of village children. As a grandmother, Jo is known as GaGa to Raizel (9), Sabryia (7), SaVaughn (4), and a newborn, Tayla Marie, expected in May of 2013.

Family and close friends describe Ms. Simpson as a woman with a generous heart, a joyful spirit, and a sense of humor. Her favorite scripture is Philippians 4:6–7, which says, "Be anxious for nothing, but in everything by prayer and supplication, with thanksgiving, let your requests be made known to God; and the peace of God, which surpasses all understanding, will guard your hearts and minds through Christ Jesus" (NKJV).